Between the Joints & the Marrow

Garrett Soucy

Fernwood
PRESS

Between the Joints & the Marrow

©2024 by Garrett Soucy

Fernwood Press
Newberg, Oregon
www.fernwoodpress.com

All rights reserved. No part may be reproduced for any commercial purpose by any method without permission in writing from the copyright holder.

Printed in the United States of America

Cover and page design: Mareesa Fawver Moss

Cover photo: Tijana Drndarski

ISBN 978-1-59498-146-3

For my children.
May your imaginations love God fiercely.
And to my brother, Gil, who started me on poetry.

Contents

Moving Day 9
Removing the Feast 10
One Hand Lying to Another 11
Brazen 12
Just Like Me 13
Son of Nun 14
A Nameless Man and His Even More Nameless Girl 16
Rootstock 18
Mandelbrot's Flower Perennially Blooms 19
Augustine's Pears 20
House (Part One) 21
House (Part Two) 22
When the Country Was New 23
On Araunah's Floor 24
Twins (Part One) 25
Twins (Part Two) 26
Darius the Dragon Slayer 27
Mouthful of Dust 28
Song of Ascent 29
Autopsy of a Moabite Stripper 31
Soft Walls 32

Mirus	33
With a Thousand Birdhouses	34
16	35
Someone Else's 16	36
Skin Fade, Hard Part	37
Going, Going, Here to Stay	38
Sacrifices	39
Ice Cream Is for the Aged	40
Renting the Church	42
My Cousin, Edom	44
Chesterton's Immolation	46
Fear and Trembling in the Annelid	47
humaN	48
Making Soup for Daniel	49
Renovation Plans	50
Four Corners of the Sheet	52
New Jerusalem Shaft Bells	53
Labor and Delivery	54
Ox	55
Lion	56
Eagle	57
Man	58
3,000 in the Furnace	59
Hyper-normalization	60
Growing Out	61
A Napkin about His Head	62
Bloody Horns	63
The Dishonorable Emperor	64
Bunyan's Oilman	65
Burning the Tartarean Sweater	66
Philanthropic Principle	67
At Nothing	68
Opening the Matrix	69
Stirring Up the Gift	70
Paper Crown	71

There Shall Be No Snare for Image Bearers 72
Captain Perfect through Suffering 73
Hell Mouth 74
Oeuf 75
Prideworn 77
Te Deum 78
An Older Recipe 79
The Book Burner 80
Rebel Box 81
7 Stars, 7 Horns, 7 Eyes 82

Moving Day

Did Eve ever talk about the past?
Did laughter ever spill out over her post-exilic teeth?
And when I woke up, God still had his mouth on my nose.
Or could Masaccio have opted to open his aperture
At any other moment
And still have retrieved an image of our mother frozen salt-still
In the grief of expulsion?
Phan Thi Kim Phuc leaving Eden,
Awaiting a greater covering.
Atonement hungry.

Removing the Feast

They carried the linens on which they sat
Stretched across the ground
Huddled together on Egyptian thread.
Small bread for many.
Dew in memory.

There were these lines of communication
Proffered vertically.
What they did they did quickly.

They kissed the rock to slake their thirst.
Lips pursed and puckered.
A woman in a hat asked
For a slice of cucumber in her glass.

This cup is not for you.

After lunch the hunt began.
Commotion erupted over whether or not
The Caterer could be found
Before it was time for tea.

One Hand Lying to Another

Acting must also be a sin,
She said, alluding to the duplicity.

But how she could belt out Eugene O'Neill
All day long without blushing.
What sent her conscience into a panic
Was her own portrayal of herself,
Her memorized lines of candor.

Rahab, we are told, acted righteously,
Though she lied.
A queen in the kingdom of God
Hiding Jews in the attic of a Jericho whorehouse.

Cunning is not condemned in Scripture; unjust harm is.
Peccable cunning will tear us apart.
Acting without truth is Jezebel's crown.
Be assured, oh, future of film,
The hand that does that kind of lying
Will inevitably grow teeth.

Brazen

They traveled from the mountain
Along the sea-coast road
That led to the house of the children's uncle.

Someone began to yell
About not listening to the right people
When making decisive turns.

The youngsters imagined it was olden days
When being lost was as good
As being abandoned by God.

The car needled through the mountains
Like a fingernail on corduroy
Stopping where the cliff had collapsed on all sides.

Everyone out.
The sun, a day-sized spotlight.
Everything getting its turn on stage.

The black, slithering bed
Moving amongst the debris
Pushed them back toward the Volvo.

Even the eldest began to shake.
"Dear God, what have we done?"
Eyes pelican-like toward the sky.

Just Like Me

Here I am as a baby in the water.

Here is my mother,
Nursing me while knowing
That I would be hers only briefly.

This is me, forced to leave home
Only to be tempered
And sent back.

Here is my laughter at the joy of finding a wife.
Here is my anger at the ways
In which she was not accepted.

Everyone wanted to eat but no one would sit down.
So, I told them to spread out in the yard
And we blessed God's wondrous provision.

Who took this one of me, at the front of the parade,
As though they wouldn't have known
Which way to go otherwise?

At the top of the hill,
The two fields intersected,
I and Thou.

Here the light was nearly blinding.
Just within earshot
The men could be heard praying.

I remember coming down
With gifts for all the kids
And wine for the adults.

Son of Nun

When the old man was still alive
He reminded them of all he had taught them.
We will remember, they said,
As though their mouths needed only make the sounds
And his shallow hopes would be pacified.

Don't forget.
We won't forget.

How boring is death to the immortal young.
He watched the young girls
Wheeling trays of triangle sandwiches
And tortillas rolled up with cream cheese and jam
Out into the great room
Which had been emptied of chairs
In order to clear a place
For people to shuffle about
Holding paper plates
And mumbling their ancient platitudes.

He's missed.
So sad.
Wonderful man.
Better place now.

Why he was left unattended
Or how he managed the strength to reach the yard,
No one knows.
The student cosmetologist hired by the funeral home
Said it took her nearly half an hour
To clean the dirt out from under his nails.

The large dug hole in the lawn was soon thereafter
Filled by a sexton in a calfskin and lambswool vest.
That single rock jutted above the ground
As the old man had done first.
He left it standing against the oak tree
Under which, with strained breath,
The man had muttered that all of his children were liars.

A Nameless Man
and His
Even More Nameless Girl

Undoubtedly most would not call it love,
What proves to be unstable
When one must fight in order to live.

The sound of laughter over wine
Under the roof of a stranger,
Groans under the blaspheming of life.

When sunlight breaks the darkness,
The danger of the streets quiets down.
The burden of care not rising on its own feet
Needs the fearful to learn to lift.

The city that gives sanctuary to pride
Forever drinks the philosopher's cup.
Gargling the tea in a debauched key.
By the end of the twelfth verse,
There are no singers left.

With skill the coward wields the knife
To make the bystanders cower.
The lines are taut where skin and bone,
Once caressed, now rot.
Sorrow-bound hands that prophesy
Are clean, punitive, and deft.

The shame-faced neighbors now
Must answer the rapping on the door.
The sons of Cain with sun and rain
Have swallowed up the sons of Seth.

There is no lifting left.
Despising her that giveth life
They pledge their love to death.

Rootstock

When my wife was a child
She would lie on her father's chest
Training her breathing
On the rising and falling of his stomach,
Trying to catch up to the man
Who had been doing it
For decades already.

Your inspiration shall be my inspiration.
Your expiration shall be my expiration.

My son tells a joke
He heard me deliver in the car.
Timing and emphasis
Fashioned in such a way
As to make the lines his own.
Round and round the airport;
Nowhere to land.

Your laughter shall be my laughter.
Your let down shall be my let down.

My mother would roll the dough thin
So that the cinnamon and sugar
Would take the stage.
I mimic the ratios even now
Not for the want of the rolls
But for that of time travel.
New patterns bowing before the old.

Your need shall be my need.
Your timing shall be my timing.

Mandelbrot's Flower Perennially Blooms

It does not close;
It just keeps opening.
In this new spring
David is not king.
Saul still wears the ring
And his kingdom only grows.

The cities of the plain
Cleared of every stone
Stripped of flesh and bone
In dust the proud lie prone.
Capernaum alone
Will surpass Sodom's pain.

Keilah in the fray
Beckons danger toward
The anointed of the Lord.
The future can afford
A molinistic cord,
For those who stop to pray.

Augustine's Pears

Craning o'er the wall
Like a child bent on seeing,
While the parapet designed to hold him back
Rather seemed to egg him on,
As though nothing could go wrong.
For a single pear the orchard would not lack.
Only borrowing, not thieving. In economy, not in being.
But his tip-toes were too stretched to break the fall.

Ask Augustine if stolen waters
Are sweeter on the tongue
Or sweeter in the belly of the rake.
Those pears are his, not any other's.
Those prayers are whispered by the mothers
Of all those takers in the war of give or take.
The fruit is passed along from the aged to the young.
And with worms about their teeth they thank their fathers.

House (Part One)

There is no misunderstanding
As to why the red duct tape
Stretches like this across the living room floor.
The house has been divided into parts
And all that we once shared
Is now the punchline to a joke
About a cubist taking a wife.

House (Part Two)

One sixth is all that remains
And even this is shaking,
Like a teenager, non compos mentis on a bridge
Who, even though her mind has changed,
Isn't sure that gravity can be avoided
Long enough to climb the netting
And feel the safety of the speeding cars
Only inches from her face.

There used to be a house here.
There used to be a garden.
Gloria Patri sounding from the rafters.
There was wine which was passed around the table.
There once was space,
But now a vacuum.

When the Country Was New

Back when the townsfolk
Would push along the edges of the road
In order to catch a view of the passing crown,
When one mouth could cast a line
Into a crowded bar
And a school of voices would follow the sound;

There is a chorus still,
Breathing in and holding,
Waiting for the hand of the conductor to come down.
There's an assembly still,
Gathering in the fringes
Of the newly wedded bride's white earthen gown.

Back when the temple
Would hum with adoration
And the hymn would echo out throughout the town.
When the men removed their hats
And with a song put forth a question
To which the women sang the answer in a round.

There is a chorus still,
Breathing in and holding,
Waiting for the harvest of the seed which has been sown.
There's an assembly still,
Gathering on the mountain
Near the canyon where the ancient grapevines are grown.

On Araunah's Floor

The long line of the barn's face
Is eastward pointed
So that the orange and vanilla sun
Can smile upon all those who greet him
When he turns over in the morning.

Someday these lines
Will accord with judgment,
With the beating of the grain.
A barn whose floor
Will then be gilded.

Twins (Part One)

While looking for the hammer
Someone took the nails
And scattered them like choke-vine seed
From the top of the wall.
Laughter retreating down the alley
As air hissed from the punctured tires
Letting the vehicles down on their bellies
Like tired Elijahs.
Give up.

Get up.
Rejoice, oh barren one.
Stand up on your feet
And take a deep breath.
He that sits in the heavens laughs.
His king is on the mountain
Disseminating kernels like a bird.
Someone take the chalk
And draw a sacred circle round the temple.

Twins (Part Two)

While looking for the hammer
Someone took the nails
And scattered them like choke-vine seed
From the top of the wall.
Laughter retreating down the alley
As air hissed from the punctured tires
Letting the vehicles down on their bellies
Like tired Elijahs.
Give up.

Get up.
Rejoice, oh barren one.
Stand up on your feet
And take a deep breath.
He that sits in the heavens laughs.
His king is on the mountain
Disseminating kernels like a bird.
Someone take the chalk
And draw a sacred circle round the city.

Darius the Dragon Slayer

Stack those boards on the trailer,
The foreman hollered from the edge of the parking lot,
Winding the long rope around a cable wheel.
Just within sight of the palace,
Where the queen was clearing table,
Where the wooden monster had been slain.
The skeleton was being dismantled.
Stack those boards on the trailer
And bring them over to Araunah's barn.
Someone will eventually lay down a floor.

Mouthful of Dust

Denial is a sure sign of guilt.
Anonymous donor.

If you hadn't broken it, it wouldn't be broken.
Fistful of wires.

Tell us the truth and we'll listen to you.
All ears.

Millions of sardines funneling in the blue,
Mirroring Vaux's swifts in the sky above the water.
Teeming hordes and lone stragglers,
Mountains above and below,
Monsters and dragons still lurking offstage.
I don't know any of it.
I have not heard the song of *Chondrocladia Lyra*.
I will remain silent.

Song of Ascent

The black night still caked like soot
In the corners of my eyes.
Sleep had left me talking to myself.

It occurred to me,
From my blanket on the floor,
To crawl across the room and find the switch.
Click.
The hum of the wires and the new faint glow.
My knees on the brown boards of the ash-wood floor.
Red splotches.
My eyes adjusting.
Clinging to the back of a dining room chair
I pulled up until all 205 pounds was stacked on my feet.
Rickety.
Trickily, I began to stand
And turned my gaze upward to the orange bulb
Hanging like a cartoon sun in the faded asbestos sky.
My throat softened under the drink.
I began to pray.

And for the start of a new day.
For the forgiveness of sins.
Thank you.

The drapes pulled back and morning honey
Poured in through the glass panes.
Yellow fire from an ancient and faraway hearth.
Snow on the ground.
White dripping in crooked lines.
Clear tears on the cold glass.

Praise him for the coffee.
Praise him for the bread.
Praise him for the strawberries and juice.
Praise him for the marmalade.
Praise him for the milk and the clean, clear water.

Autopsy of a Moabite Stripper

When they opened up her belly
The carcasses of undigested men
Poured out onto the table
Like berries in a partridge's crop.

More still had calcified
On the skin around her breasts.
Heads burrowed into her pores
Looking for God only knows what.

She has a lovely face, he said
As the hydroaspirator slipped from his hand
Banging on the reflective steel tray
And landing on the floor.

They just keep coming.
The only thing to do is to let the stream run
Until there are no men left
And then sew her up.

The intern declined the offer
To see for himself that her neck and chin
Still smelled like cinnamon and hay.
Suit yourself,
But don't complain to me that the room smells bad.

Soft Walls

It's good for a man
Who spent the day lugging mud and bricks
Up the ladder to the first level of staging
To be allowed to have both elbows on the table
Guarding his food and hulking his mouth closer to the plate
So that the reward won't take so long,
So that the reward won't be taken.
It's good for the waitress to bring him another
Beer without him having to ask for it.
It's good for him to push his chair back
When the plate is white again
And to have it disappear quickly
And a hot cup of tea steaming in a saucer
Placed where his hand can touch the porcelain
In order to see if it's ready to drink.
It's not good for man to be alone.
Not when the pub is full of clinking glasses
And occasional pops of laughter.
It's not good for a man to be alone.
Not on a canvas of fellowship.
A monosenochlotic oddity.
Like the solitary woman in the blue Honda
Who has just burst into tears
Turning out of the Walmart parking lot.
Her anguish is visible because of the light,
Not in spite of it.

Mirus

When you are old enough to dream but still too young to marry
All the wonder that has been gathered up off the forest floor
Is deposited in anticipation of the future feast.
Little wooden swords unable to pierce
Mock the future heros
While pirates maraud
The earth.

Someday, the doors will open;
And the halls will echo with the songs of warriors.
The trays of lamb will emerge from the kitchen,
Six at a time and then some.
The singers will call for attention
And with warm breath, glorified with mead,
The tale will be told of one who moved
From the kitchen to the battlefield to the throne.
And all the women will move from their seats
Locking arms in the kinetic knitting of the knot
Until the linen and lace
Appear to be folds upon folds
In a single garment.
A photonic meta-gown.

We are eating even now,
Boys and future women
Pulling from the same bread,
Fingers in the same cup.

With a Thousand Birdhouses

When my father's father was a boy
This tree had only one swing on it.
Each time it returned to center, the tire dragged in the dirt.
Then, the first time the house burned, it took the tree with it.
Look at it now, all bursting with swings
And a thousand birdhouses.

16

The reason he was told he could never marry was that
The people might cheer.
They might throw rice and wave
Along the steps leading up to the church.
There might be kisses on the cheek and hands firmly clasped.
Men might offer to buy the groom a drink,
Hand the man a cigar,
Or sabotage his car.
His children would want to play and run through the yard
Into the neighbor's driveway.
And that mustn't happen—
For the sake of the children,
For his wife,
And for his own heart.
Those who rejoice when the Lord is blasphemed
Will break their teeth on the wind.
The Lord no longer mourned the dead;
He could not celebrate the living.
He could not allow him to marry
Because the pain of loneliness would be gentler
Than the anguish of undoing.
There would be no corner of the white gown
A living man would venture to touch.
Soft teeth like stones disappearing amidst the gravel.
Bridal hair, ribbons and all,
Divided amongst the wake,
Carried away by the kettle.

Someone Else's 16

I never married.

But this was someone's wife, once.
Scratch that. It was someone's bride.
Parts of the schäppel could be seen
Sticking out of the mud.
Nearby, a vulture's face was hidden
By the black lock in its beak.
A portion of the strands thinly braided
And matted at the broken end.

It would have been better to have never married.

Skin Fade, Hard Part

All the men leaned forward as the voice emerged
From under the steaming cloth.
The only sounds competing with the story
Were the heavy breathing of the barber
As he wheeled around the chair
Turning his patient as he moved
And the metal scrape of the scissor spring.
The talking planet.
The clipping satellite.
Wheels within wheels.

That ain't nothing.
Her little sister was fixated
On only one thing...

What?
They all knew, but they wanted to hear it.

On raising the bar. Or lowering it.
Her sister died in the care of those boys.
The paramedics said you could see her bruises through her shirt.

The barber peeled back the now cold cloth
Like a man unmooring himself from a tub long since drained.
There was only brown stubble where a mane had once flickered.
The Navy man with the unfolded newspaper looked out the window:

Looks like that bird is pulling a branch out of the ground.
Or maybe it's sticking it in.

Going, Going, Here to Stay

Children love it when the illustrator
Fatigues the boy hero
By having him climb for hours
Up the curvature of the mountain
Only to reveal, three pages later,
That the mountain
Is the shell of a giant turtle
Or the back of a sleeping dragon.

Well, in this case,
Come to think of it,
It's something similar.
That smooth stone—
Taken so long ago from the brook
By the hand of a young boy
Which levels the scaled dragon
In the Valley of Elah
—that smooth stone
Is shown to be a mountain
Three pages later,
When the boy moves
From the kitchen to the battlefield,
To his, eventually, having a mountain of a son
Who fills the whole earth.

Sacrifices

Someone left out the bottle of wine
And everyone went to bed.
Brettanomyces set to work
Like a secret elf.
It was three days later
When we finally made it home.
The boy, first in the house,
Dropped his bag on the counter,
Corked the bottle
And put it in the cupboard.
That evening during the meal
It was served to the guests.
The quieter man of the two,
With the napkin on his lap,
Pushed out his chair and rose.
Parts of the water-damaged ceiling fell around
The table, like dripping porridge as he spoke.

What is to be done with a stubborn animal?
Can it be ignored that the pasture is rejected?
Can I laugh with you at dinner,
While your wife's hand billows the table skirt
To touch the mayor's leg?
I will not.
Your cup is defiled
Like your well and your bed.
Tell the young bride
She has vomit on her veil.
The wind hath bound her up in her wings,
and they shall be ashamed because of their—

Ice Cream Is for the Aged

In the bed by the window
A white-haired man breathes
The blue light in and out.
When he wakes, he will move
To the desk near the door
And sketch out plans
For the spring garden,
Just as he saw it
When it woke him;
Just as it will be
When he does not see it.

On the first floor,
His granddaughter is mumbling,
Indiscernibly at first,
And then clearly
As she breaks into song.

For he that is mighty hath magnified me:
And holy is his name.
And his mercy is on them that fear him:
Throughout all generations.

The morning cook leans her back against the wall
And weeps with gratefulness into her apron
While the rest of the house sleeps.
Kitchen tears salt her mouth.

Outside the cankerworm and caterpillar
Have eaten the trees bare and back again.

A mortal wound is sopped
With the white of the moon
And the sign of the cross
Is drawn with ash
On the forehead of the sun,
That well of fire
Which causes the pink cosmos to bloom
When the spheres are properly ordered.

Renting the Church

The good news is the funeral
Doesn't start until four;
So there is plenty of time
To move folks over to the reception hall
Before the mourners arrive.

Everyone wants to walk through
The big wooden doors
And the stone archway.
Everyone wants their voices
Echoing and imprinting
Into the six hundred years of ceiling.

This young girl
Who will be carried across a threshold
This evening
Will, on another evening,
Be carried across the one she now walks over.
The white veil she wears
Is black over the face of the 4 p.m. wife.

O eternal God, Creator and Preserver of all mankind,
Giver of all spiritual grace, the Author of everlasting life:
Send thy blessing upon these thy servants.
Thou knowest, Lord, the secrets of our hearts;
Shut not thy merciful ears to our prayer;
But spare us, Lord most holy, O God most mighty,
O holy and merciful Savior, thou most worthy Judge eternal,
Suffer us not, at our last hour, for any pains of death, to fall from thee.

As the celebrants move in a long white row
Out the vestry and across the yard,
An older woman stops to rest on the Gethsemane Bench.
She will need to move faster
If she does not want to be confused
For a member of the party of mourners
Weaving in a black line through the front
Door, sniffing and short of breath.
She watches with keen interest as
A hauled moldboard, across the street,
Threatens to overtake the combine.

My Cousin, Edom

You watched the blue lights
From your third-story bedroom window.
When the vehicles had left
And the help had gone home
You descended like Carter's vulture
To taste the carrion for yourself.
The front door was left open
And so you walked about the house
Dumping drawers,
Turning on lights,
And running the water.

You left the refrigerator ajar revealing that
Not even the baking soda remained in the freezer.
Moths began to gather
Around the dining room chandelier
As you roamed the house
Like a slacker come prepper
Whose smirk and dishabille
Lend credence to the instability.
Eating sandwiches
And drinking tea
That someone else had made.

You will not be allowed to keep your room
When the movers begin to unpack.
Someone let the mortgage default and there is no cure.
The debt has accelerated beyond recognition.
Laugh as much as possible.
Drink the last of the whiskey you can't pronounce.
Stand in front of the mirror and flex
Like a boy with only time to spend.
Headlights in the driveway.
Feet pounding the walkway.
Someone's at the door.

Chesterton's Immolation

The most scenic vista
If you really want to watch the city burn in style
Is going to be *Lover's Lane*
Which is the road that ends at the edge of a cliff
Just across the bay.
You can watch it all happen in living color
While a few people kiss in their cars.
Be careful if you walk along the path to the benches,
Near the scrub pine,
Because tiny *pyrus cajon* seedlings have begun to sprout
And the smallest rustling
Could possibly dislodge their fibrous roots from the topsoil.

Fear and Trembling in the Annelid

Despite the shaking of the ground
It is the direction of the light
And so the setae
Catch and release:
Rings of round ribbing.

His weight upon the earth
Is not the presence of his adding
But the wonder of his taking:
Forgiving iniquity;
Anger dissipating.

We, the humble by design,
Not curse. Mouths of dust.
Prostomium.
Proskuneo.
Walled in by castings.

God's mighty hand and omnipotent arm
White and shriveled from salt spray,
Wet and withered,
Back from the erasure
And now empty.

humaN

In this city, the taxis are red
And even though the streets are wide
They jostle each other like competing electrons.

In this city, the rivers are wide
And climb over their banks
To gulp away the edges of ancient buildings.

In this city, like competing glances,
The radios stop blaring the crooners' promises
As the cars are swallowed up by the esurient pools of fire.

There is no healing the bruise of such a grievous wound.
Once you were the spitting image of the crown.
Now you are the stench of rot within the cavity.

Making Soup for Daniel

My contention is not with the help, but the management.
His knife flew furiously through the air
And clapped on the cutting board like a tap dancer,
Over and over. Bits of onion fell overboard onto the counter.

He spun the cap off the glass jar, too quickly,
And shook the hard green leaves over the steaming pot.
Too many bay leaves and now the soup would be bitter.
My contention, he repeated, *is not with the help, but the management.*

This is your restaurant. Let it fail if that's what you want to do.
And quietly the response came, which included
Examples that proved the point that, far from failing,
Management, rather, was doing all that was necessary to keep it open.

The kitchen doesn't know where the books are kept,
Let alone how they are managed.
Now, pick some more of those leaves out. Add some honey.
And take Daniel his lunch.

Renovation Plans

It's not just this town
With its melting domed roquefort frittata
On a cauliflower crust
Served on a plain white plate.
It's all the other towns
Up and down the coast
That hum with their low frequency
Adorno and Horkheimer steamers.

Not one massage parlor will be left standing.
The farmer's market will be turned back
Into pasture and the sheep will not remember
The dye-free shopping bags
For which their wool was once harvested and spun
To carry the stick of butter and shot of cream sherry
From the co-op to the Tesla.

Not one art gallery will be left standing.
The Dutch antique shops will become true
Remnants of the useful past their present prices
Now mock. Poor women will once again
Rock in those chairs, while their fingernails
Chip away at the Quebecois milk paint finish.
Chifforobes popping off their rosewood tops
Out in the sun, out in the yard will be laid
In the dirt and fashioned for box gardens.

And God will put a pure language
In the mouth of a new people.
They will not shrink back from the edge of the word
But will honor him with lips prepared for praise.
All along the coast, he will gather together
Those who were silenced by the solemn sentencing
And he will weave their chains into mail
And their sorrow into joy.
Glimmering in song along the morning coast, they will
Shine like the sun in the kingdom of the Father.
Then, he will break new ground.

Four Corners of the Sheet

What will change
On that day when the heavens
And the earth shall be shaken
In order to make more room for that which
Cannot be shaken?

We watched it change.

Two women,
One at the end of her life
The other at the beginning,
Both framed by twelve years for Israel.
Both in trouble because
Life is in the blood
And one or the other was leaving.

We watched it change.

If one bear holy flesh in the skirt of his garment,
And with his skirt do touch bread, or pottage, or wine,
Or oil, or any meat, shall it be holy?
And the priests answered and said, No.

We watched it change.

Andres Serrano's crucifix
Thrown into the waters of Marah
In order that the thirsty might drink,
That the hemorrhaging might cease,
That the dead might rise in time for breakfast,
By the pure and purifying finger of God.

New Jerusalem Shaft Bells

Holy unto the Lord.

Taxis everywhere.
Crotals and shaft bells fill the air.
When the frothing horses stand still, note the short inscribed prayer:

Holy unto the Lord.

Holy unto the Lord.

The donkey and colt in tandem make fine procession fare.
Children leap into the road, their
Voices fill the square.

Holy unto the Lord.

Labor and Delivery

In the early blue-gray hours of the morning
Of the northern hemisphere's vernal equinox
The pasture-side door of the milking parlor
Had been left open, and Trudy sauntered out.
Her twin watched from the far side of the fence
As she walked away from him
And the overturned cup roof
Of the blood-red grain silo.

Two days later, when the boys had ridden to the pits
To shoot Rich's new rifle, something caught
Henry's eye, and he turned the wheeler about,
Eastward, facing the limestone ledges.
He would later tell the vet,
*She was all scrunched up on the limestone bed
Like a furry black question mark
Splattered on the rock.
I thought she's dead.*

The farmer pushed the word *anastomosis* toward the vet
As if folding a winning hand down on the table.
There was no conversation to be had
About a freemartin calving, let alone
Calving alone in the woods and surviving.

The black and white critter wobbled to its feet
As Pritchard took a towel from one of the boys
And began to wipe blood, mucus, and dung from his arms.
The calf kicked its back feet at the same time
And stood still for a moment, arching its neck in the air.
He's looking for his father, the vet said
And then shook his head as if he had swallowed a bee.
I mean his mother. I don't know why I said that.

Ox

Alter not the ancient boundaries
And so provoke the Lord.
He has set the winds in circuits.
Tidal edges have been hemmed along the shore.

Little stot, why then your lowing?
Why your noises in the night?
Know ye not his teeth are worthless?
Here the shadow has no substance in the light.

Have ye not a joyful service,
Bringing tribute to your king?
Stretched and bound upon the altar,
Be ye cheerful, little priest, in your ascending,

Lion

Put the wine upon the table
While brandishing the sword.
Put an answer to the riddle.
Let the young receive the wisdom of the word.

Little proud one, why your pacing?
What do your noises say?
One amidst the coalition
In which leadership is proven in the fray.

Have ye not a fearsome stature,
Made a mirror to your king?
So love virtue as you govern.
In your reigning shall be singing and bell ringing.

Eagle

Looking back and looking forward
Like the rusted and the spry,
Like a face before a mirror
Where it's possible to look in one's own eye.

Little raptor, why your chirping?
What are your noises for?
One amidst the convocation
In which vision is established as you soar.

Have ye not a sober vision,
With insight from your king?
Be ye joyful in ascending.
Wise hearing is the wearing of a prophet's earing.

Man

When I was young,
I stood in the crowd and demanded
That we be given Barabbas.
When Pilate waffled I echoed what was said,

His blood be on us and on our children.

These days I find myself
Praying those same words with newer zeal.
Only knowing the weight
of what is meant by such a strange appeal.

His blood be on us and on our children.

This is how the kingdom
Is taken, by force and with thanksgiving.
My son hears the *Gloria Patri*
And, from his high chair, he perks up and sings.

His blood be on us and on our children.

3,000 in the Furnace

Turn aside to see this thing.
There are men upon the altar
And yet they do not burn.
They are the nations of the earth.
The ground on which they stand
Is holy unto the Lord.
There will be no shoes in glory.

Hyper-normalization

Ellul once said that the need of the hour
Was mutants, not separatists.
I would beseech you
By the mercies of God,
And not the evils of technology.
It is the presentation of our bodies
That must take place,
Not merely the living in them.
But we must live in them
In order to present them.
It is either conform or transform.
There is water that is word,
The application of which changes the form.
I've been accused of being brainwashed.
To which I say,
Amen. Thanks be to God.

Growing Out

Some lives are spent
Not knowing why one is weeping,
Growing tired of waiting around for dinner,
And moving one's body in such a way as to find pleasure points.

A mumbling round man
Forgets to lock his car and is able
To pull the fob from his jacket as the horn honks two
Short reports without him having to even dismount from the recliner.

It's possible to buy
A sippy cup from the gas station
That will hold over one liter of soda. Refills cost less
Than a dollar. The man asks if the machine has milk or only soda.

Moving his body in such a way as to find pleasure points,
Growing tired of waiting around for dinner,
He spends his life not knowing
Why he is weeping.

A Napkin about His Head

What is this fig leaf
Behind which Moses hid
In order that the people might not know
That the glory was fading
Into the end of one covenant
And the beginning of another?
It is a veil that is removed
When inviolable glory is seen.

How does one see it?
One sees with one's ear.
How does one believe it?
By opening one's ear.
Who can open the ear?
The One who speaks.
What is that sound?
It is the sound of a veil
Being removed, folded, and set aside.

Bloody Horns

Ears thou hast bored.
Blood from the lobe, from the thumb,
From the toe, and in circumcision.
Thou hast laid hold of the horns of the altar
And hidden thy word in the heart of the mountain.

Saints are those permitted to now pass through the curtain.
And pass through we have, as on dry land.
There is a preputial record of past wrongs
Cast into the sea of forgetting.

But do you, O Master of All,
Declare this water to be water of redemption,
Water of sanctification, a cleansing of flesh and spirit,
A loosing of bonds, a forgiveness of sins,
An illumination of soul, a laver of regeneration,
A renewal of the spirit, a gift of sonship,
A garment of incorruption, a fountain of life.
For you have said, O Lord:
Wash, and be clean; put away evil from your souls.

The Dishonorable Emperor

Teetering on the porch,
On the edge of another break,
Wielding the pages of Scripture
Like hexagrams of the I Ching.
Hemmed in on either side
By a parapet of two lines
Desperately needing to be proven complementary
Or the relationship must end,
Or the furthering of the universe
Would be threatened.

How did the vertical and horizontal
Beams of the cross not harmonize
Opposing forces?

Railing against the thought,
He moved to the ground.
I can climb the mountain.
But don't make me carry the wood.

Bunyan's Oilman

House after house on this lonely stretch of American village
Is perched near the side of the road like a white, wooden layer hen.
Blue light flickering in its glassy eyes. No eggs.
The snow reflecting the photonic static,
Evoking a response from inside the car as we inch
Our way across the county.

It's beautiful. The blue light from the windows
Blinks on the banks like the moon has scattered
Its seed in the yard.

Perhaps it is beautiful because the car has trapped
The sound of the monks of the Chevetogne Abbey
Conducting vespers for our pleasure, at our whim.
We listen like gluttons, not even praying, though professing belief.
Perhaps it seems beautiful because it is Christmas, and we know
The child will be crucified. Everything glints a kind of beauty.

The light is cold and contrasted by the other windows seeping
Yellow and orange honey into the night. A laughing man stands
Next to a table where his friends are ladling soup and covering
Their own laughing mouths. It is gilded and warm and the forms
Are true. Living souls, not frozen frames, change the shape of
The waves. There is beer on the table and another tall man
Leans in his chair and turns the damper in the stove pipe.

Perhaps it is because, in the car, everything comes through a screen.
Perhaps Pascal was right and we cannot see the beauty
Without mediation. We don't deserve museums.
Give us Bunyan's oilman, secretly stoking the flames which are
Threatened with extinction by all the cool, lunar images
Flashing through the glass in medias res.

Burning the Tartarean Sweater

At times it is as though the lamb is pulling
At threads in the sweater, somewhere far beyond,
Where the shearer missed a spot,
Where the carder didn't finish,
And the spinner forgot to cut. The lamb.
The dark and almost invisible moire threads.
Pulling at that over which it still claims ownership.
We sit, like strange creatures, part ape, part lamb,
Curious as to whether or not these unlit spots at which we pick
Will shed clean, or open up greater holes which we will
Not know how to fill. One who looks like the Son of Man
Holds a white linen garment, folded, in his hand.
Put it on.
There is the imprint of his face on one side. It bleeds
Through the cloth. It is tight and feels as though
It is scraping our skin. With new eyes, we look
In an eternally young light to see a squirming mass of ash
Littering the floor around our feet. His face, like a mirror,
Shows one lingering cross where the ash does not fall,
Centered on our foreheads. The debris begins to congregate,
Taking our forms upon itself and migrating home.
What do we do?
He holds up his hand, and the muscles in our arms
Flicker.
Kill it.
Ash to the fire.

Philanthropic Principle

Through the walls of water,
Pits of lions,
Hordes of snakes,
And desert wanderings.

Through the walls of Jericho,
Pits of traitors,
Broods of vipers,
And desert temptations.

God is expressing his will upon his people,
Like patrons at the bar who are offered free peanuts
In order to create a demographic in the market for beer;
So, God is willing to incite a drought in order to build up a thirst.
A logos drought. A word famine.
If anyone is thirsty, let him come to me and drink.

At Nothing

Fear is the orchard of the enemy.
Eat nothing that is cooked with those apples.
Drink not his cider nor his wine.
The color is vivid, as red as the cinnamon
In the mouth of Phryne.
The smell is cloying, as lush as the sweetgrass
On which Sada Abe is sprawled.
You must listen for the sound
Of the worms devouring the flesh
And leaving only excrement in their bored channels.
Let no one deceive you.
Fear is not of God.

Opening the Matrix

A crown for the girl who has loved
The hearing of the word
More than the restating of it.
The perseverance of faith,
The abidance in holy charity,
The soundness of mind—
And she is saved from repeating the past.
For this reason, and more, wisdom is personified as a woman,
Because she is a mother, whose nourishment will not only
Impart a godly application of knowledge, but will give life.
Fitting, since she is the mother of all the living.

Stirring Up the Gift

Brings it to the surface.
Fear is a sedentary stillness,
Which causes it to sink to the bottom.
It was given by the laying on of hands;
And so it should be in your hands,
On the edge of being given,
As gifts are want to do.
Not hidden in the heart of the mountain.

Paper Crown

What makes it blasphemy?
Being slow to acknowledge the sacred.
How is the word of God blasphemed?
When grandmas are drunk,
When discretion is shunned,
When the home is despised,
When obeisance is disdained,
It is blasphemy.
It is blasphemy because an older woman
With a silver crown
Is called a sacred thing by the word,
And she who wears the crown should be sanctified.

There Shall Be No Snare for Image Bearers

Look at the man, ploughing in lines,
As though the horizon were a guide to draw by.
Look at the birds, picking seeds from the ground,
Only to be caught in his net.
Look at the silver fish, jeweled and writhing
Like living waves crashing against the wall of the seine.
Notice what ought not be here, worked into the soil
Of given dominion. There is no man
To be planted and plucked up
Like Ruby Queen Hybrid by a flesh and blood combine.
Let all the earth rejoice,
Says the crown of all creation.
Let everything that hath breath praise the Lord.

Captain Perfect through Suffering

Spray-painted in white block letters on an overpass
On the outskirts of Bethlehem reads the line,
BABIES ARE MURDERED HERE.
Little boy blue, loaded in the station wagon
And tasting death for all people.
Plotting, even then, a revenge
That was the sole business of his father.
Death would die for this and more.
The oily residue, bitter on his tongue;
Over his mother's shoulder, he could see
The dragon swinging its tail through the little town.
Under it's forearm was a glass spot, not covered by the scales.
One could see the serpent's heart, slowly heaving back and forth
Like a crow on a swing in a cage. Even then,
As the taillights of the car rolled toward the Egyptian border
He could feel the earth shaking under the collapse
Of the near future falling.

Hell Mouth

High above the earth, where the little drone is safe to hover
The red fire rages like a prison riot. Even at these heights
It is impossible not to imagine the black plastic heating up.
Moving in along the coastline, where the water is holding
Its hand against the orange fray, a ketch is banking hard,
Bringing it about and heading for home. A frantic boy runs
From the edge of the woods and into the house, slamming
The screen door and tossing a lighter into the kitchen trash.
His neighbor's kitchen window is open and the sound of
A marriage ending is flung upon the sidewalk and parts of
The abutting yard. Some words cannot be unspoken. Like
A cast-iron pan midair, they drop, they do not fly from the
tongue.

Oeuf

In the blue light of the cutting steel
Of a winter's night, a sedan slowed
As I walked a pace between where I had
Been and where I was going. Cheek by
Jowl, the window of the passenger side
Rolled and emitted a howl. Folks who,
No doubt, would pledge their fealty, were
Headed to the lake to run cars on the ice.
Run with us,
They said and wondered at my demurral.
It's cold outside. Come sit by me.
Her eyes were a heavy, drunken blue glass.
The warm air spilled into the street with
The sticky breath of Quelques Fleurs. Her
observation made the wind blow harder
Until I touched the silver handle and
Nearly climbed in. The snow crunched
Like corn starch on linoleum beneath my boot.
You go on. I want to walk.
The sweet heat, the beckoning back seat,
The smoke wisps lifted into the air from a crack
On the driver's side like a message about the pope.
I joined its procession
And whispered a petition.
You go on. I want to walk.
And with that turned my back on the chance
To shrink time and end suffering. To awaken that
Which had been sleeping the sleep of death.
The engine roared. The taillights blinked and dissolved.
Shoving my hands deeper into my coat, I found
The last hard-boiled egg that remained from lunch.

With frozen hands, the shell was peeled, peppering
The snow until the warm white sphere looked back
At me from the palm of my hand like all the
Tomorrows of eternity.

Prideworn

Fear runs on pride so much of the time
Because the ground is so far from the sky.
We are tree-house dwellers out of season.
God's hand is heavy and it rests on the ground.
Safety is under it, not above it.
Humus. Human. Humility.

Te Deum

Love is burning with the light
From Lewis's sun, not only seen
But having all things seen by it.
We harness the light that has come
Trillions of miles in order to watch
Reruns of *Night Court*. It ought not
Be this way, and yet, there are two
Prodigals in the parable: two men
Who wantonly waste it all. Each holds
An opposing end.
Each is willing to spend lavishly
On people who do not deserve it.

An Older Recipe

If you remember my letter from a few years back,
The one in which I suggested altering the recipe
With the introduction of coriander, remember,
You agreed to try the alteration but refused to
Make a note, even in the margins, lest you be guilty
Of the worst kind of redaction? I'm writing now to
Tell you about what happened to me this week. As
Is my custom, I stopped in to John's little book closet
On the way home from the gym. He had set aside a
A muslin-bound 1800s reprint of *The Forme of Cury*
Which he thought I might be interested in. I was. When I
Got home, before turning in, I was thumbing through
The pages when a card from the Parker House Hotel
Fell to the floor. Upon closer inspection, I noticed
On the back, scribbled in pencil, was a page number
And the word *Cormarye*. Upon locating the reference,
You can imagine my surprise when the recipe called for
Coriander, spelled *Golyandre*. This, my dear friend,
Clears your conscience, I hope, and cheers your heart.
That which we have both thought of as a new thing is in
Truth, a very old thing.

The Book Burner

Beginning to write,
I find that the very thing
Trying to be put into ink,
Can only be put into space.
When we speak face to face,
Words wasted on food and drink
Are alone the ones we are living.
In the end, the words were rite.

Rebel Box

There is a box full of rebel angels,
Set aside for moving day.
Planetless satellites.
Raging sea waves.
Foam and spray.
Some have wandered
Near the lid
And found themselves within.
Pull one from the clenching grip
And head back in again.

7 Stars, 7 Horns, 7 Eyes

Early morning, I rose and wandered about the house,
Not being able to sleep any longer. The stillness,
The clean floors, the new clothes—it would take
A while for these things to become the new normal.
I came into the kitchen, looking for a glass, but not
Wanting to wake the others, I leaned down and drank
From the faucet. The water was charged with air and
Felt like sea spray. I stared at the faces on the refrigerator
And saw a note addressed to me and the others. It stated
That the food was to be eaten. The wine was in the cellar.
When our host returned, we would dine together. If we were
Willing, would we set out chairs on the patio for the guests?
There was a list of names, but the writing had become illegible.
The numbers were clear, and so I opened the drapes,
Sat down at the table, and pulled out my phone. A timer beeped.
Coffee began to drip into the double-walled carafe. The lights
Crept on, and music could be heard on the second floor. Someone
Was drawing a bath in the nearby washroom. A child was sliding
His way down the staircase on his bottom. The wheels of a car
Crunched the crushed rock in the front driveway. Soon, there were
Bacon and eggs, milk in clear pitchers, oranges being pressed, and
Cream put in mason jars and set in bowls with ice. He had already
Begun making calls. I had risen when others came in, so I sat again.
They're on their way. Should be here shortly. They're bringing fish.
I pulled out my phone and looked at the list. There were ten digits,
No dashes. Assuming the one who answered wouldn't recognize my
Number, I introduced myself and explained the background noise.
Tall kitchen. Bright chrome. Clean counters. Yellow tiled floor.
Uh—um. I believe you're expected for dinner.

Title Index

Symbols
3,000 in the Furnace 59
7 Stars, 7 Horns, 7 Eyes 82
16 35

A
A Nameless Man and His Even More Nameless Girl 16
A Napkin about His Head 62
An Older Recipe 79
At Nothing 68
Augustine's Pears 20
Autopsy of a Moabite Stripper 31

B
Bloody Horns 63
Brazen 12
Bunyan's Oilman 65
Burning the Tartarean Sweater 66

C
Captain Perfect through Suffering 73
Chesterton's Immolation 46

D
Darius the Dragon Slayer 27

E
Eagle 57

F
Fear and Trembling in the Annelid 47
Four Corners of the Sheet 52

G
Going, Going, Here to Stay 38
Growing Out 61

H
Hell Mouth 74
House (Part One) 21
House (Part Two) 22
humaN 48
Hyper-normalization 60

I
Ice Cream Is for the Aged 40

J
Just Like Me 13

L
Labor and Delivery 54
Lion 56

M
Making Soup for Daniel 49
Man 58
Mandelbrot's Flower Perennially Blooms 19
Mirus 33
Mouthful of Dust 28

Moving Day 9
My Cousin, Edom 44

N
New Jerusalem Shaft Bells 53

O
Oeuf 75
On Araunah's Floor 24
One Hand Lying to Another 11
Opening the Matrix 69
Ox 55

P
Paper Crown 71
Philanthropic Principle 67
Prideworn 77

R
Rebel Box 81
Removing the Feast 10
Renovation Plans 50
Renting the Church 42
Rootstock 18

S
Sacrifices 39
Skin Fade, Hard Part 37
Soft Walls 32
Someone Else's 16 36
Song of Ascent 29
Son of Nun 14
Stirring Up the Gift 70

T
Te Deum 78
The Book Burner 80

The Dishonorable Emperor 64
There Shall Be No Snare for Image Bearers 72
Twins (Part One) 25
Twins (Part Two) 26

W
When the Country Was New 23
With a Thousand Birdhouses 34

First Line Index

A
A crown for the girl who has loved 69
Acting must also be a sin 11
All the men leaned forward as the voice emerged 37
Alter not the ancient boundaries 55
At times it is as though the lamb is pulling 66

B
Back when the townsfolk 23
Beginning to write 80
Brings it to the surface 70

C
Children love it when the illustrator 38
Craning o'er the wall 20

D
Denial is a sure sign of guilt 28
Despite the shaking of the ground 47
Did Eve ever talk about the past? 9

E

Early morning, I rose and wandered about the house 82
Ears thou hast bored 63
Ellul once said that the need of the hour 60

F

Fear is the orchard of the enemy 68
Fear runs on pride so much of the time 77

H

Here I am as a baby in the water 13
High above the earth, where the
   little drone is safe to hover 74
Holy unto the Lord 53
House after house on this lonely
   stretch of American village 65

I

If you remember my letter from a few years back 79
I never married 36
In the bed by the window 40
In the blue light of the cutting steel 75
In the early blue-gray hours of the morning 54
In this city, the taxis are red 48
It does not close 19
It's good for a man 32
It's not just this town 50

L

Look at the man, ploughing in lines 72
Looking back and looking forward 57
Love is burning with the light 78

M

My contention is not with the help,
   but the management 49

O
One sixth is all that remains 22

P
Put the wine upon the table 56

S
Some lives are spent 61
Someone left out the bottle of wine 39
Spray-painted in white block letters on an overpass 73
Stack those boards on the trailer 27

T
Teetering on the porch 64
The black night still caked like soot 29
The good news is the funeral 42
The long line of the barn's face 24
The most scenic vista 46
The reason he was told he could never marry was that 35
There is a box full of rebel angels 81
There is no misunderstanding 21
They carried the linens on which they sat 10
They traveled from the mountain 12
Through the walls of water 67
Turn aside to see this thing 59

U
Undoubtedly most would not call it love 16

W
What is this fig leaf 62
What makes it blasphemy? 71
What will change 52
When I was young 58
When my father's father was a boy 34
When my wife was a child 18
When the old man was still alive 14

When they opened up her belly 31
When you are old enough to dream
   but still too young to marry 33
While looking for the hammer 25, 26

Y
You watched the blue lights 44

www.ingramcontent.com/pod-product-compliance
Lightning Source LLC
Chambersburg PA
CBHW010046090426
42735CB00020B/3407